# 30 DAYS TO BLAZE

A practical guide to getting unstuck,
finding your fire and igniting your life!

## JASON BARNABY

Copyright © 2019 by Jason E. Barnaby

All rights reserved. This book or any potion otherof may not be reproduced or used in a ny manner whatsoever with the express written permission of the publisher except for the use of brief quotations in a book review.

Printed in the United States of America
First Printing, 2019. ISBN: 9781729845110
Published by Kindle on Demand Publishing.

# CONTENTS

Introduction .................... **7**

Day 1: Differentiate .................... **10**

Day 2: Question .................... **12**

Day 3: Uncover .................... **16**

Day 4: Define .................... **18**

Day 5: WhatIfAbouts .................... **19**

Day 6: Name .................... **20**

Day 7: Own .................... **21**

Day 8: Dare .................... **22**

Day 9: Investigate .................... **23**

Day 10: Refresh .................... **25**

Day 11: List .................... **27**

Day 12: Defining .................... **30**

Day 13: Geometry .................... **31**

Day 14: Three .................... **33**

Day 15: Torch .................... **34**

Day 16: Mission .................... **35**

Day 17: Research .................... **37**

Day 18: Inquire .................... **38**

Day 19: Combine .................... **39**

Day 20: Action .................... **40**

Day 21: Tribe .................... **42**

Day 22 Inventory .................... **43**

Day 23: Admire .................... **44**

Day 24: Hire .................... **45**

Day 25: Fire .................... **46**

Day 26: Council .................... **48**

Day 27: Engage .................... **49**

Day 28: Revisit .................... **50**

Day 29: Prepare .................... **51**

Day 30: Tribe On! .................... **52**

Inventory .................... **54**

Definitions .................... **55**

# INTRODUCTION

**Hello Fire Starter!**

Yes, I'm talking to you.

If you have purchased this book, received it from a fellow tribe member or picked it up because you are curious about the title, you **ARE** a Fire Starter. I know you. Maybe we haven't met face-to-face, but I know why you have this book in your hands. In one way or another, you are stuck.

You know there is something better "out there." You can feel it and it's nagging at you—whispering, calling and beckoning you to come along on a new journey. You're curious. You may even let your guard down enough to dream just a little. To ask yourself "What if?"…

The problem with that what if question is that it lets all kinds of other thoughts and fears in. It's kind of like this. You are on one side of a valley and can sort of see the other side. It's not really clear, but you know it's there and **there** is where you want to be. How do I get there, you ask? What's the first step? What's after that? Is there a map?

The answer to that last question is YES! You are holding it. 30 Days to Blaze was born out of my collective of experiences including:

- A mediocre undergrad career
- Serving as a founding member of Indiana University Dance Marathon
- A 2-year stint as a "professional" ski bum
- 8 years living and working in Poland
- Graduate school that lead to a 20+ year teaching career
- A failed venture as a coffee shop owner
- 10-year corporate career encountering hundreds of stuck people
- Running a marathon
- Writing my first book, *Igniting the Fire Starter Within*
- Launching Fire Starters Inc. as a solo-preneur after my corporate job was eliminated

I call 30 Days to Blaze the road map out of "stuckedness."

What's the scariest thing to overcome when you are stuck? If you are anything like the people I've met during my adventures around the world, it's **getting started**. You may have heard the old adage about how to eat an elephant…one bite at a time. Well it's the same with getting unstuck. Except instead of bites, its steps.

This program is designed for you to make one intentional step every day for 30 days to lead you from the land of stuck and suck to the land of freedom. Along the way, you will discover who's in your tribe, get feedback from them, do a self-assessment, face down those nagging fears, create a personal mission statement and throw a party to celebrate the journey.

I grew up hearing my dad say over and over, "If you aim for nothing, you'll hit it every time." Specific goals with intentional outcomes produce positive change. You have taken that first step by opening this book. Committing 30 days to your growth and development is specific and intentional and **will produce** the change you have been looking for.

By opening this book, you've struck the match. The next step is to start the fire and watch it grow as you work a little each day on becoming the person you were designed to be. As you do so, you will cross that valley—one step at a time—and before you know it, you'll be on the other side. The good news is, you're not alone. I'll be here with you every step of the way to guide you. Feel free at any time while you are completeing this journaling workbook to email me: jason@firestarterstribe.com or call/text me at 317-709-4104. I'm serious. I want you to succeed and start living the life you were made to live.

Welcome to the Fire Starter's journey!

Tribe On!
Jason

## DAY 1
# DIFFERENTIATE

*"If you can't figure out your purpose,
figure out your passion. For your passion will lead you right into
your purpose."*
**– T.D. JAKES**

*"Chase your passion like it's the last bus of the night."*
**– UNKNOWN**

I'm so excited for you to start your Day One exercise. Before you start, though, here are two rules you will follow when completing each daily exercise. Please read them out loud and initial them if you agree to follow the rule.

**1.** Get comfortable being uncomfortable. If you're not willing to do this, close the book and give it to a friend. I'm serious. Outside of your comfort zone is where growth and change happen. If you aren't willing to be uncomfortable and challenge your status quo in this process, you won't change.

I agree to follow Rule #1 as I complete each daily exercise_____(initials)

**2.** Do not filter your wild ideas or "inner child." This workbook is all about becoming that version of you that you dream about. Your purpose. Your passion. Your dreams. Truth is, though, you're stuck in fear and doubt and uncertainty and comfort.

I agree to follow Rule #2 as I complete each daily exercise_____(initials)

**Empathy vs. Passion**

These two are often confused. I've defined them below to help you differentiate.

**Empathy** is seeing a need or a cause and feeling compelled to put your time or money behind it because you feel it. It moves you. You go to a fundraising event and give money. You see a commercial about hurricane victims and give money. You volunteer at a homeless shelter at Thanksgiving. It might fire you up, but it doesn't consume you. These acts fill your want to "do something." In short, you see the need, you give time, money or resources and you move on.

**Passion** has shades of empathy, but it's a different level altogether. Passion keeps you up at night and energized during the day. You read about it. You watch about it. You subscribe to it. You research it. You talk about it to people around you. It may be all you talk about. It could be a hobby, your vocation, or the thing that should have been your major in college. The difference here between passion and empathy is passion has that *something* you just can't shake.

The distinction between empathy and passion is crucial for what truly sets you on fire. Experience says that coming face-to-face with your passion can be scary. Even so, you are still drawn to it.

**DO ⇢ Below, fill out the two lists while keeping in mind the rules above and the definitions for both empathy and passion.**

**What I'm empathetic about:**

**What I'm passionate about:**

## DAY 2
# QUESTION

*"The art and science of asking questions is
the source of all knowledge."*
**– THOMAS BERGER**

*"The important thing is not to stop questioning; curiosity has its
own reason for existing."*
**– ALBERT EINSTEIN**

Today is all about questions. Make sure to carve out some time with no distractions to think about your answers.

**DO ⇢ Answer the following questions with whatever comes to mind. Use an additional sheet of paper, if necessary, to capture all your thoughts.**

**Who inspires you? (mentors, thought leaders, family members, bosses etc.)**

**Why? What characteristics do those people possess that inspire you?**

**What inspires you? (nature, accomplishment, possessions, travel etc.)**

**Why? What is it about those items you listed that inspire you?**

**What activity or activities make you come alive? This may come from particularly fond memories you have doing something as a child.**

**What need do you see in your world that you think needs to be filled. You find yourself saying, "someone should do something about that."**

**What do you share on social media (snap chat, FB, Twitter, Insta)?**

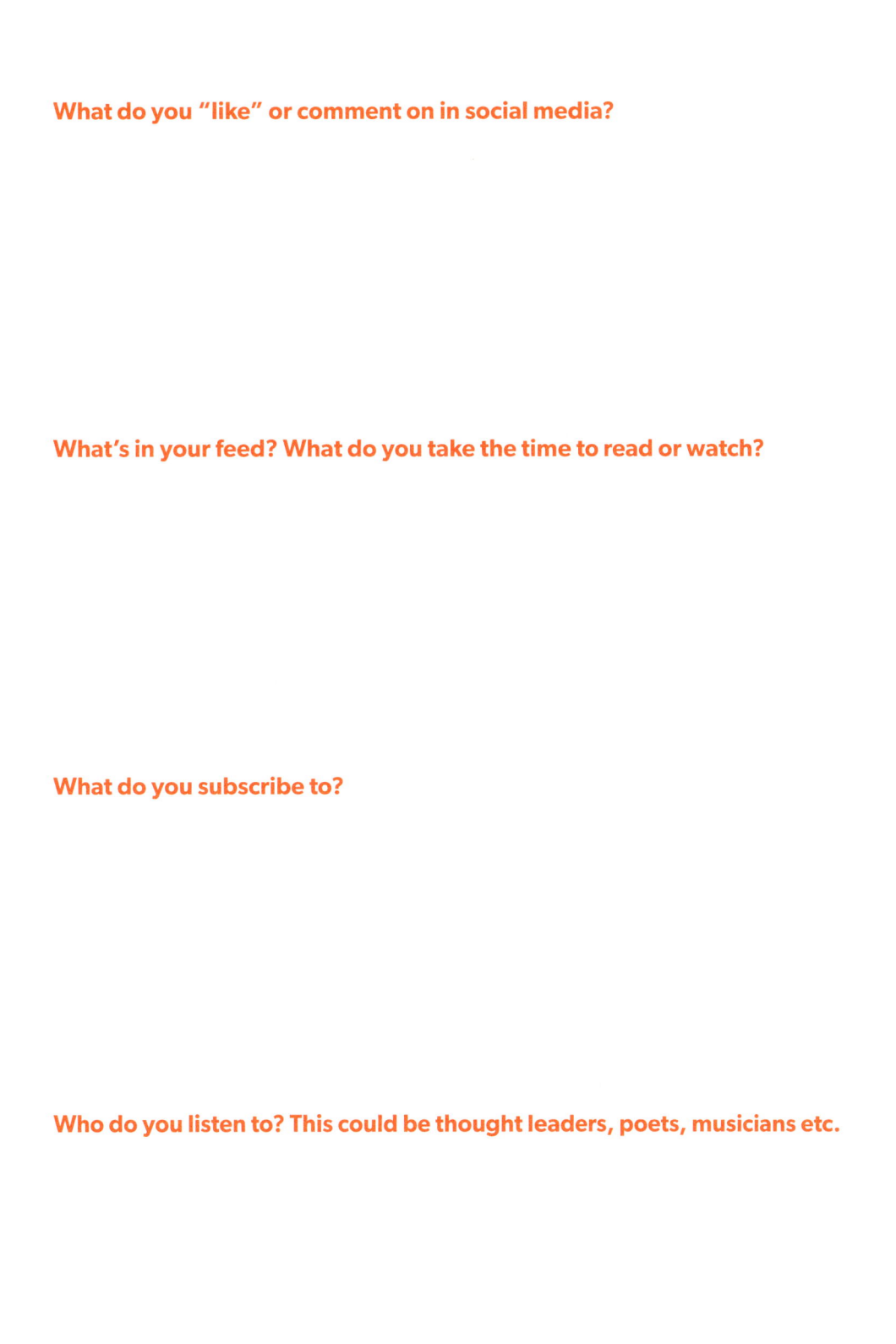

**What do you "like" or comment on in social media?**

**What's in your feed? What do you take the time to read or watch?**

**What do you subscribe to?**

**Who do you listen to? This could be thought leaders, poets, musicians etc.**

**What do you dream about? This could be a dream while you sleep or a daydream while you're awake.**

**If money were in abundance, I would come alive…(think about what a great day might look like in this scenario)**

**If time were in abundance I would come alive…(think about what a great day might look like in this scenario)**

# DAY 3
# UNCOVER

*"At the intersection where your gifts, talents, and abilities meet a human need; therein you will discover your purpose."*
**– ARISTOTLE**

> **DO** Answer the following questions with whatever comes to mind. Use an additional sheet of paper, if necessary, to capture all your thoughts.

**What do other people say you are good at?**

**What do others seek your advice on?**

**How do you spend your free time? How would you like to?**

**What patterns/themes are consistent in the answers? Do those make sense? Why? Why not?**

**Do they surprise you? Why? Why not?**

**My ideal community is...**

**What about the place above makes it ideal? What can you do there? What draws you there? (weather, activities, geography etc.) What kind of people live there?**

## DAY 4
# DEFINE

*"At the end of the day, you can't control the results; you can only control your effort level and your focus."*
**–BEN ZOBRIST**

**DO ⇢ Go back and review your questions and answers from Days 1-3. As you review, continually ask yourself these questions:**

**What is my fire?**

**How does my current life look next to the life I want?**

### DAY 5
# WHATIFABOUTS

*"Avoid head trash. Don't be a garbage can for anything that does not feed your intellect, stimulate your imagination, or make you a more compassionate and peaceful person. Refuse to open your mind to other people's trash. Tune out anything that promotes conflict or controversy. This can infect you with a mind virus of cynicism or defeat, and you won't even know it!"*
**–LES BROWN**

In all my travels and various jobs in my life, I have met many, many people who are prisoners to the doubt and fear that exists (almost completely) in their own mind. I made up a word and dedicated a whole chapter it.

**WhatIfAbouts**
1. The conscious and unconscious space we get stuck in that is full of fear and doubt and precludes/prevents/blocks/obstructs our forward progress.
2. The head trash that plays on repeat about past problems, current short-comings and future failures.
   Here are some examples:
   *What are you thinking? Who are you to try that? What makes you so smart? Someone else is already doing that That will never work! Dumb Idea.* You get the picture.

The point here is to be aware of their existence. I'm almost certain some of them showed up yesterday when you were defining your fire. That's normal. The WhatIfAbouts will fight hard to keep you stuck.

But don't worry! I'll teach you some strategies to combat the WhatIfAbouts in the coming days.

**DO ⟶ Be aware that the WhatIfAbouts exist and pay attention to when and where they show up.**

\*\*Optional exercise\*\* Go back and revise the answers to your Day 4 questions based on what you now know about the WhatIfAbouts.

### DAY 6
# NAME

*"We are each gifted in a unique and important way. It is our privilege and our adventure to discover our own special light."*
**– MARY DUNBAR**

The time has come! We've "danced around the flame" long enough. Time to put a name on it. What is it that makes your heart catch fire? You've had it running around in your head for the last five days. Time to put it down on paper.

**DO ⟶ Write down the name of your fire. It may or may not be what you expected. That's okay! You may need to wrestle with it still. That's okay too! How does it feel to see it on paper? Are you surprised? Why or why not?**

## DAY 7
# OWN

*"Own your fire!"*
**– BRANDY HOLLAWAY**

Yesterday you got your fire out of your head and onto paper. Today we go a little deeper with it. Why does this particular thing set you on fire? Where does it come from? Dig in.

**DO ⇢ Use voice memos on your phone, talk to yourself in the mirror or do some more journaling here to unpack and articulate why this is your fire? Think of it as the business "elevator speech." Can you clearly explain what your fire is, where it comes from and why it's important etc. in 30-60 seconds? That's your goal for today.**

## DAY 8
# DARE

*"First, think. Second, dream. Third, believe. And finally, dare.*
**– WALT DISNEY**

Today you are stepping into potentially unfamiliar and uncomfortable territory. Dreaming. Somewhere on the road to becoming an adult we lose this ability. It's not generally welcome in tall buildings and conference rooms. We are often too busy with life, work, kids, house, or family to waste time on silly dreams. Well, today you are going to do just that, but it is neither a waste of time nor silly.

Allow this to be uncomfortable. This is where the growth happens, remember? Also, the answer will not be in your phone, so put the phone in airplane mode or set to 'do not disturb' for 30 minutes and put it down.

**DO ⇢ What is a dream you have? Think about: where you are, who you are with, what you are doing, what is the process, what is the outcome? Write it down. Write it all down.**

**What are the WhatIfAbouts that come with it? Write them down, but don't give them much more attention than just writing them down and then move quickly back to dreaming and daring.**

## DAY 9
# INVESTIGATE

*"I think it's very important to have a feedback loop, where you're constantly thinking about what you've done and how you could be doing it better."*
**– ELON MUSK**

Have you ever heard the saying "feedback is a gift?" It's true, but that doesn't mean you don't want to return the gift from time to time…

Some of the workshops I lead focus on feedback. I find that there is always a higher percentage of people that want to GET feedback compared to those who want to GIVE feedback This is partly because people don't know how to ask for feedback and partly because people don't know to give it without hurting the other person's feelings.

I've developed a quick and easy system that takes the awkward out of asking for and receiving feedback. You can also use it at work with other teams in your company, your customers, or your peers. It's called five by five plus one (5X5+1)

> **DO ⤳ Ask five people to give you five adjectives that describe you--four positive and one you need to improve. This is the 5X5 part. Have them give you context for the word--what they mean or an example where they saw it evident in your life. Context is key. It will help you see how they see you.**

Now for the "plus one" (+1). Do this same exercise for yourself BEFORE you get any feedback from the five people. If you wait, you won't be honest with yourself. I recommend writing down your five words with context before you send out the request to your five people.

Give them a week to complete this for you. Follow up at the midpoint of the week as a reminder. Once everyone has responded with their words, compile a master list that includes your five words for a total of 30 words.

The next page is numbered 1-30. Use it to make your list. If you get a word more than once, write it again so you fill in all 30 blanks. DO NOT spend the time you have after writing these down to ONLY focus on the "needs improvement" words. Seriously! Don't do it!

1.

2.

3.

4.

5.

6.

7.

8.

9.

10.

11.

12.

13.

14.

15.

16.

17.

18.

19.

20.

21.

22.

23.

24.

25.

26.

27.

28.

29.

30.

## DAY 10
# REFRESH

*"Time spent in self-reflection is never wasted—it is an intimate date with yourself."*
**– UNKNOWN**

**DO ⤳ Go back and review days 1-9 to remind yourself of your fire and the WhatIfAbouts that come against that fire. Pay attention to the WhatIfAbouts and start to ask yourself where they come/came from. Use the space below to brainstorm, reflect or journal.**

# JOURNALING
**DOODLING SPACE**

## DAY 11
# LIST

*"Learning too soon our limitations, we never learn our powers."*
**– MIGNON MCLAUGHLIN**

Our WhatIfAbouts come from a variety of sources—parents, teachers, colleagues, bosses, spouses, children, siblings. Some may even have come from complete strangers. There is no denying their existence, or their power. They can cripple the mind, and in turn cripple the body. They are responsible for getting us stuck and keeping us there. I hate them. I really do. I have seen so many people keep their gifts and talents locked in a vault guarded by fear and doubt as result of the WhatIfAbouts.

Conversely, I've seen people bust through these fears with boldness and courage and realize that most if not all of the fear and doubt was simply in their mind. Turns out, the WhatIfAbouts are really just paper dragons. You know what conquers paper dragons right? We'll get there soon enough…

**DO ⇢ Fill each of the columns appropriately.**

- **Column 1: Name**
  Identify a WhatIfAbout and write it down
- **Column 2: Origin**
  Think about where it came from. Did it come from a particular person? A particular situation? Maybe it's founded in fear and doubt you've created in your mind. Fill this column in with the origin of the specific WhatIfAbout
- **Column 3: Reaction**
  How does this WhatIfAbout make you feel? Does it discourage you? Cause you anxiety? Does it cause you to have doubt or fear in regard to your ideas and abilities?

Here's an example of one for me. I had a teacher in high school geometry that told me I was unteachable. I got my only D in my entire academic career (through grad school) in his class.

| WhatIfAbout | Origin | Reaction |
|---|---|---|
| You suck at math. How can you run a business if you don't do math? | Math teacher in 9th grade | I feel stupid and intimidated by math so I often don't try. |

Now it's your turn. You may or may not need two pages, but you have it if you need it. Take your time with this. Allow yourself to be uncomfortable. Growth… Remember?

**WhatIfAbout** | **Origin** | **Reaction**

**WhatIfAbout** | **Origin** | **Reaction**

## DAY 12
# DEFINING

*"You cannot learn very much about excellence from studying failure."*
**– MARCUS BUCKINGHAM**

*"The only limitations you will ever have are the
ones you put on yourself."*
**– KRISTINNA HABASHY**

After taking an inventory of your WhatIfAbouts, their origins and your reactions, it is likely that there are some "front runners" that are more consistent or prevalent on that list than others. Often these WhatIfAbouts have defined your character and personality and how you have lived your life. You may be afraid of vulnerability because you are afraid people won't like the "real you." As a result, when people get close, you get mean to keep them away.

What are 3 "defining" WIAs that have been constant in your life? It's possible you don't have three, but I doubt you have less than two. Again, as an example, here are mine.
1. You don't have anything to say
2. You're not qualified to speak with authority on anything
3. You're basically an imposter and one of these days the truth is going to get out

These show up for me when I'm in a meeting pitching Fire Starter Inc. services, when I'm preparing a keynote and when I'm getting ready to step on stage.

Here's the good news. Since I know what they are, and I've written them down, they don't swirl around like a cloud of chaos in my head. I have also learned to recognize their tactics and when they tend to show up, so I'm more aware of them and how to fight them. This didn't happen overnight, and I still struggle. It takes work and this is where you start your work to fight back.

> **DO ⇢ For now, let's focus on your "defining" top three and where you believe they came from. List them below along with their origin. We will complete an activity with these three in a few days. The most important step today is to get them out of your head and onto the paper.**

1.
2.
3.

# DAY 13
# GEOMETRY

*"Only acknowledge your limitations for the purpose of overcoming them."*
**– RANDY GAGE**

You got your feedback for the 5X5+1 on day 9. Today you will dig deeper into that feedback by putting the words into three categories. Instruction for that are below.

**DO → Put a circle** next to the words that you expected to get as feedback—these are words typically related to your strengths.

**Put a square** next to the words that surprised you that people noticed—these are words that could be hidden talents or talents you knew you had but didn't think others noticed. Whatever the reason, you were surprised to see them on the list.

**Put a triangle** next to the ones that "need improvement." You will be tempted to beat yourself up about these words. Don't! We all have areas we can improve. You should constantly strive to learn and grow and never get (or stay) stuck! Knowing these trouble areas gives you specific targets to focus on for improvement.

Once you have completed this exercise and **put the correct geometric shape next to each word,** you will have a visual of your strengths and also areas that need improvement. It's possible you've discovered skills to use that you aren't using currently or ones you could further develop that you aren't using to your full potential.

**Now comes the work.** Change doesn't happen in a week or a month. Forming new habits takes time and intention. Below write down a word from each category that you will continue to focus on along with a time commitment. At minimum, you should choose one month. I suggest three months—especially if a new quarter is about to begin. That's an easy way to track the time. But don't wait for a new quarter before you start!

Additionally, **find someone to hold you accountable** for the action plan you devised for those words.

Strength I'm aware of (Circle word) _____

Time Commitment (length of time you will focus on this) _____

Start date _____

Accountability partner _____

Unexpected Strength (Square word) _____

Time Commitment (length of time you will focus on this) _____

Start date _____

Accountability partner _____

Needs improvement (Triangle word) _____

Time Commitment (length of time you will focus on this) _____

Start date _____

Accountability partner _____

# DAY 14
# THREE

*"Many of us feel stress and get overwhelmed not because we're taking on too much, but because we're taking on too little of what really strengthens us."*
**– MARCUS BUCKINGHAM**

Go back to your Day 9 list and choose your three greatest strengths. What have people always told you you're good at? What have you been noticed or rewarded for in your life? What do people turn to you for advice on? These may be a skill you bring, a perspective you have, or an action you can spark.

**DO ⤑ Top three strengths. Write them down below. After you have written them down, use the extra space to brainstorm some ways these strengths are related to or fit with your fire.**

**Strength #1**




**Strength #2**




**Strength #3**

## DAY 15
# TORCH

*"Torching your fears is simultaneously igniting your dreams."*
**– JASON BARNABY**

Today we play with fire! You didn't think I'd start a company called Fire Starters Inc. and not include the use of actual fire, did you? I don't mean actually play with fire, but we are going to use it (with proper safety precautions in place) to ignite action!

> **DO ⇢ You'll need six index cards or pieces of paper the size of index cards**
> - **On the first three index cards, write down the 3 WhatIfAbouts form Day 12.**
> - **On the next three index cards write down contrary evidence to each of those.**

**Example:** If your WhatIfAbout says that you are a failure, write "You are a failure" on one index card. For contrary evidence, on a different index card, write down, "I'm not a failure b/c I have achieved (insert list of achievements)."

Once you have all 6 index cards filled out TORCH the three index with the WhatIfAbouts. Keep the other three and post them on your bathroom mirror as a reminder of your strengths and a way to fight back against the WhatIfAbouts.

**Be careful to do this in a fire pit outside, over a sink, or over a bowl of water. Always have a pitcher of water on hand just in case.**

Get creative! Blast your favorite music, open a special bottle of wine, toast with your favorite food or beverage, dance around the room, high five your bestie. The sky is the limit!

### DAY 16
# MISSION

*"Perhaps the most important vision of all is develop a sense of self, a sense or your own destiny, a sense of unique mission and role in life."*
**– STEPHEN COVEY**

Hopefully by now, you are starting to gain some clarity around your strengths and areas of improvement, along with your fears and where they come from. All of this should be stirring your ember and fire inside. Likely, your development, your dream life, and your individual purpose are taking up more and more of your head space as you continue to think about and work on you.

This is where the WhatIfAbouts love to wage a counterattack. You've torched the big ones and you're getting better at seeing when and where they like to attack. Today you will set an intentional plan to keep the momentum going.

**DO → Write three action statements based on what you have accomplished thus far in the 30 Days to Blaze program.**

**Examples:**
- I will manage my time better and not waste time on social media by logging my screen time daily
- I will watch an inspirational video every day on YouTube to keep my mind and heart engaged
- I will revisit my plan for development weekly and track my progress on strengths as well as weaknesses

Use "I will" statements for these. They need to be activities that you will actively do, not something you are going to stop doing. Additionally, include **HOW** you will do this as I have done in each of the examples above.

**Active mission statement #1**

...............................................................................................................................

**Active mission statement #2**

...............................................................................................................................

**Active mission statement #3**

## DAY 17
# RESEARCH

*"The biggest adventure you can ever take is to live the life of your dreams."*
**– OPRAH**

Today is all about giving yourself permission to explore! Based on what you are uncovering and discovering about your strengths, fears and original design, take today to do some research on topics that interest you. Here are some simple and easy suggestions for where to start:

- Your company's job board
- Your company's volunteer/community involvement opportunities
- Organizations that support or are supported by your local church, or the school your kids attend
- Go to Facebook or Instagram or LinkedIn (or all of the above) and search people or hashtags related to what you are interested in and subscribe to their feeds
- Coaching a local sports team
- Leading a youth group
- Your own thing you've been thinking about since you started reading this list

> **DO ⇢ Lastly, do a Google search for non-profits related to your fire. What are they? Can you join them? How? Non-profits are rich in passion and drive, but (often) poor in organized talent, strategy, leadership and resources. What could you bring to the table that they are lacking? It's amazing the response when you reach out and ask how you can help.**

## DAY 18
# INQUIRE

*"Let's get comfortable being uncomfortable, shall we?"*
**– JASON BARNABY**

Are you ready to uphold that Comfortable Being Uncomfortable promise you made on Day 1? I know you are! Today is all about putting **ACTION** to your planning and research.

Based on what you found from your research, it's time to inquire. This is scary. The WIAs come swooping in here like a tsunami. What if they think I'm crazy for asking? Who do I think I am anyway? This problem is huge, what can I do? What if nobody responds?

As scary as this is, it is **essential** for you to take this step against your fears.

> **DO** ⇢ **Put out a feeler to your social network asking if people know of organizations like X (an organization that you found in your research) that need Y (that thing that is your ember).**

You will likely find two things to happen when you do this:
1. Your network is watching
2. Your network has suggestions

The above leads to the realization of two truths:
3. The WhatIfAbouts lose power as you stand up to them
4. Everything you want is on the other side of fear

## DAY 19
# COMBINE

*"Pay attention to the things you are naturally drawn to. They are often connected to your path, passion and purpose in life. Have the courage to follow them."*
**– RUBEN CHAVEZ**

I tell my tribe all the time that it is **not necessary** for you to abruptly quit your job, sell all your possessions and go in search of this thing that sets your heart on fire. No!

When you begin to engage your heart and soul and mind in what you do every day, there will be a difference in the way you behave. You'll be happier. You'll have more patience. You'll be more willing to help others. Your approach to work, projects and deadlines will be more positive.

When your soul is filled with what satisfies it, that fullness spills over into other parts of your life.

Today is all about finding ways that your ember could be combined with action. This action will benefit you and the people/organization you decide to serve.

**DO ⟶ Answer this question: Can I combine what I love with serving/volunteering/being on a board? If so, what could that look like? If not, what else could I do to take action on my ember?**

# DAY 20
# ACTION

*"A dream written down with a date becomes a goal.
A goal broken down into steps becomes a plan. A plan backed by
action makes your dreams come true."*
**– GREG REID**

Fire Starters Inc. is all about **INSPIRED DOING**. You can plan and journal until your hand cramps and your pens run out of ink, but without **ACTION**, it's only words on a page.

Now is the time to put very specific action words on the page with very specific dates related to when those actions will be checked off of your to-do list.

**DO ⇢ Write down three distinct action steps with due dates/timeline based on days 16-19.**

**Below are a few examples**

### Action #1
Contact the local YWCA (or other community organization) to see about coaching youth soccer (or other sport or volunteering)
**Due Date:** By first Friday of the month

### Action #2
Schedule lunch with Joan and find out if she needs a board member with my skill set OR if she knows of any other boards who might need that skill set.
**Due Date:** By middle of the month

### Action #3
Watch at least one video a week (Ted Talk, Instagram TV story, YouTube) related to my ember to keep me focused and inspired
**Due Date:** By the end of the month

**If necessary, break these bigger steps into smaller steps to help you see the progress.

**Action #1**




**Due Date #1**
**Accountability Partner**

........................................................................................................................................

**Action #2**




**Due Date #2**
**Accountability Partner**

........................................................................................................................................

**Action #3**




**Due Date #3**
**Accountability Partner**

# DAY 21
# TRIBE

*"You'll need coffee shops and sunsets and road trips. Airplanes and passports and new songs and old songs, but people more than anything else. You will need other people, and you will need to be that other person to someone else—a living, breathing, screaming invitation to believe better things."*
**– JAMIE TWORKOWSKI**

*Surround yourself with people who make you hungry for life, touch your heart and nourish your soul.*
**–UNKNOWN**

We are not meant to do life alone. A tribe of people to encourage you, keep you accountable, challenge you and walk alongside of you is essential. I started a group called Tribe Vibe that receives three weekly emails from me—Monday Morning Motivation, Hump Day Hacks and Friday Freestyle. If you're interested in joining the TRIBE, you can do so at my website. www.firestarterstribe.com There is a 100% no-spam guarantee.

**DO ⇢ Write down the names of those who are currently in your tribe. Think of people that have encouraged, challenged, inspired and connected you. These are people you would call at midnight when things fall apart, and you need support. These are people who know you well. They don't have to be people you have known forever, but they could be.**

**MY TRIBE—write the names of your tribe members below**

## DAY 22
# INVENTORY

*"You are the average of the five people you spend the most time with."*
**– JIM ROHN**

For the next four days including today you'll be working in a tool I developed over several years in the many jobs I've had. It's called **The Tribal Inventory**. It identifies seven quintessential members of an effective tribe with their descriptions and has three stages. You will begin the stages tomorrow on Day 23.

I encourage you to take one day for each stage and don't rush into completing it all in one sitting. Take your time. Think about your tribe. How do they support you? Or not? How do they challenge you? Or not? Is your relationship mutually beneficial? Or one sided? Don't worry if you don't have any names listed in a one or several roles, or WAY too many in another. You may even have a few people fulfilling multiple roles. Don't sweat any of that…that's what the inventory is for.

**DO ⤑ For today, you are simply reading through the descriptions on pages 55-59 and labeling the members of your tribe that you wrote down yesterday for Day 21. Some of your members may have more than one label. That's fine.**

# DAY 23
# ADMIRE

*"Sometimes people are beautiful. Not in looks.
Not in what they say. Just in what they are."*
**–MARKUS ZUSAK**

Today you will be completing the first of the three stages of The Tribal Inventory—the Admire stage. The people you will identify in this stage are what I call your "midnight tribe." These are the people you would call in the middle of the night if you needed them and they would answer! Think about who has been a faithful and productive member of your tribe.

Here's what I've learned about these people. They are reliable. They often don't think about "being there" for you, they just are. We often assume these people know they are in our midnight tribe, and maybe they do, but often they don't.

Here's the thing—whether they know or they don't, today is the day you remind them or tell them for the first time that they are your midnight tribe.

**DO ⇢ Go back to pages 55-57 and fill in the Current Tribe Member(s) column of each role with the name or names of people in your tribe that fit that description.**

**BIG DO ⇢ Take the time to call, text, email, or stop by and let that person know that they are part of your midnight tribe. A word of caution. Make sure to tell them about this program and that you are contacting them as part of today's assignment. They may be (more than) a little caught off guard if you don't.**

As a result of today's exercise, you may realize that you have several people in each role, a few people that show up in a few different roles, or (as some of my clients have discovered) no people in any of your tribal roles. Any of these or some other outcome is perfectly fine. Tending your tribe takes time and effort and this may be the first time you have ever intentionally looked at who's in your tribe. Take it one step at a time.

## DAY 24
# HIRE

*"Your vibe attracts your tribe."*
**– UNKNOWN**

After completing the Admire stage of The Tribal Inventory, you are now ready for stage two—Hire. It is likely that you had some gaps in your Tribal Inventory as you filled in the blanks for the different roles. In this stage, you will identify people to fill those gaps.

Don't let those gaps intimidate you. One thing I have learned in my own tribe and in the tribes of those close to me, is that people like to be included and their opinions found valuable. People like to be asked to be in your tribe. A question I often get related to this stage is, "Where do I find people to be in my tribe?" The answer? Anywhere and everywhere!

Look around. Do you have kids? Do your kids do activities or play sports? Do you spend time around a lot of parents whose kids do the same things as your kids? There are a lot of potential tribe members right there. Other places to look include the company where you work, the church/worship community you belong to, the neighborhood you live in, the gym you go to. One place I have used often to add to my tribe is LinkedIn.

Lastly, think about the people in your life currently. Do you have someone who could fill that role currently in your life? If so, call them up, explain what you are doing and ask them to join your tribe. You just might be surprised by their answer. You don't know, though, until you ask.

Yes, I know this has the potential to stir up some anxious thoughts, but remember what you signed up for on day one? Say it with me! Comfortable being uncomfortable.

**DO ⇢ Go back to pages 55-57 and fill in the Hire column of each role with the name or names of people that you need to hire in a particular role in your tribe where you have a gap.**

# DAY 25
# FIRE

*"Dealing with people can be difficult. Not dealing with them can be worse."*
**– ANONYMOUS**

Don't get nervous about this stage. If you have completed the first two stages well, the Firing stage should go smoothly. Let's be honest here. We all have people we can think of that we would like to fire from our tribe from time to time. What you want to think about here is who has *consistently* underperformed, overcriticized or just plain missed the mark. These may be people you make excuses for and have been doing so for years. That's one possibility. If you have a person or people in mind, they need to be fired from your tribe.

A second possibility is this. Is it possible that the role you have tried to put this person in is not the role they are made to play? One such scenario I find where this rings true is with Devil's Advocates and Dreamers. I'm a Dreamer. I have some Devil's Advocates in my life that I've tried to dream with and guess what? It NEVER works. They are not wired to be Dreamers, they are wired to find the holes in the dreams. Conversely, I'm not wired to find the holes, I'm wired to dream! So, it may be that you need to "fire" someone from one role in your tribe and hire them in another.

How does this look practically? For either scenario above, it looks like not engaging the people you are firing when you normally would. It looks like not responding to a text from someone in this category right away when you are bothered and not in the best frame of mind. It can also look like letting the call from "you know who" go to voice mail and then leaving it there for several hours so it doesn't derail your day.

**Your Electronic Tribe**
In addition to firing these unproductive and critical members of your tribe, you also need to tend your electronic tribe and get rid of similar "voices and influences" in your social media feeds. I'm amazed at how much we allow toxic messages into our eyes and minds on a daily basis through social media. I can almost guarantee that if you look through your various social media feeds you will find at least 5 accounts you can unfollow or delete. Conversely, you should be able to find at least 5 accounts you can add to your feed that will pour fuel on your fire.

**DO ⇢ Go back to pages 55-57 and fill in the Fire column of each role with the name or names of people that you need to fire from a particular role in your tribe where they are not supplying what you need.**

**DO MORE ⇢ Go through your various social media feeds and unsubscribe/unfollow any accounts/people that are not productive and positive influences in your tribe.**

## DAY 26
# COUNCIL

*"Call it a clan, call it a network, call it a TRIBE, call it a family. Whatever you call it, whoever you are, you need one."*
**– ANONYMOUS**

*"Find a group of people who challenge and inspire you, spend a lot of time with them, and it will change your life."*
**– AMY POEHLER**

You did it! You spent the last five days being ridiculously intentional about who you surround yourself with. You've admired your midnight tribe. You've found gaps and made plans to fill them. You've gotten rid of toxic influences—both physical and digital. This is your TRIBE. More specifically, this is your TRIBAL COUNCIL. These are people you will look to when times are hard, when times are great and everything in between. Lean on them. Ask them for feedback and do that often. Spend time with them. Share life with them.

**DO ⇢ Look back over your Tribal Inventory and think about how you could utilize each person there to help you fuel your fire. Think also about how you could show your gratitude by serving them in some way. What does that look like?**

Reach out to any people in your Hire columns and ask them to join your tribe.

## DAY 27
# ENGAGE

*"When you find people who not only tolerate your quirks but celebrate them with glad cries of 'Me too!', be sure to cherish them. Because those weirdos are your tribe."*
**– UNKNOWN**

It's time to engage this crazy band of weirdos you've decided to surround yourself with. The answer I hear so often to the 'how are you' question, is this. BUSY! I know we all have lots on our plate. I also know that we can make time for what we really want to make time for. I also know and see that we are more connected electronically as a culture and world, but also lonelier than ever. The physical meeting together and sharing of food, drink, laughter and space is good for the soul.

**DO ⇢ Contact the members of your tribe and set a meeting. You could do it at a local coffee shop, brewery, restaurant, city park, or your home—whatever fits the vibe for your TRIBE.**

This should be fun and enjoyable, not overly serious and anxiety provoking. Some general talking points could include:

- What you've been up to as you've gone through this program including what you've learned, what's challenged you etc.

- Why you're asking for this meeting—to share your journey, to ask for help or accountability or both

- How long the meeting will last—an hour is generally a good chunk of time to ask people to commit to

- What you're hoping to get from those in attendance—some will dream with you, others will keep you accountable, and still others will help connect you to others

### DAY 28
# REVISIT

*"Plan your work for today and every day. Then, work your plan."*
**– MARGARET THATCHER**

You may have found over the last month that you are TRYING to be more intentional with goals and action plans, but life has a way of getting in the way. That's normal. You are not alone in the half-crossed off list.

To help with this, today is a day to revisit your action plan from Day 20. How is it going? Do you need to make some changes? Redirect? Refocus? Today is a day for you to do that.

**DO ⇢ Revisit your action plan from Day 20 and make any necessary adjustments. Don't beat yourself up for what you've missed. Give yourself some grace and space to make the changes that need to be made.**

## DAY 29
# PREPARE

*"Success occurs when opportunity meets preparation."*
**– ZIG ZIGLAR**

**DO ⇢ As the date for your Tribal Council meeting gets closer, spend some time thinking about the meeting. Visualize what room you will be in and who will be in that room. Visualize the energy you will bring to the room. Maintain an openness to the varying opinions and perspectives that will be there. Be open to learning from each member of your Tribal Council. Be prepared to share your vision, ask questions, and LISTEN.**

Maintain an attitude of gratitude for where you have come over the last month and how wonderful it is to be surrounded by these people.

## DAY 30
# TRIBE ON!

*"Tribe On! To challenge, inspire, connect and grow."*
**– JASON BARNABY**

Congratulations! Today is day 30 and you have officially completed the 30 Days to Blaze program. As I've said a few times throughout this 30 days, Fire Starters Inc., at its core, is all about INSPIRED DOING. If you subscribe to my email list, you will see that the mantra of those emails is the "Tribe On!" quote above.

This program was designed to:

- **challenge** your comfort zone and comfort level
- **inspire** you to stop settling for a less than average life
- **connect** you with a TRIBE that will hold you accountable
- **grow** your ember into a fire you can no longer ignore

I'm proud of you for making it this far and for doing some deep work on yourself and your tribe. You are ready for the next step. You have momentum and I want to plead with you to keep going!

The world is hungry for your gifts and your talents and I'm excited to hear about your next step.

**DO ⇢ Take some time today to review all that you have done and written down in your journaling notebook during this program. Be proud of what you have accomplished.**

**Send** me an email: jason@firestarterstribe.com and tell me about your experience with this program. I want to hear praise and/or criticism. It's the only way this program will continue to improve.

**Send an email or text** to a friend and recommend this program to them. I would also love it if you posted on social media about your experience and would be especially grateful for a recommendation.

**Sign** the FIRE STARTER'S DECLARATION page below. Take a pic of it and use it as a background for your phone, tear it out and hang it somewhere you will see it often.

**You can find me on:**
    **Facebook:** Jason Barnaby—Fire Starter
    **Instagram:** firestarterstribe
    **LinkedIN:** Jason Barnaby
    **Twitter:** jason_barnaby

**Other Fire Starters Inc. services:**
I work from three main buckets.

1. Conference keynote speaking—I specialize in interactive and engaging keynotes for small, medium and large audiences
2. Corporate team packages—half-day, full-day or multiple day team off-sites or customized multi-session packages to develop leaders
3. Coaching—group and individual coaching packages available based on needs

Interested? If so, email me at jason@firestarterstribe.com or call me at 317-709-4104.

Thank you again for trusting me with your time, money and dreams throughout this program. You have found your fire, fanned your flame and tended your tribe!

You. Are. Ready.
Tribe On!
Jason

## I AM A FIRE STARTER

I'm living for…
**DEEP CONNECTION**
**INTENTIONAL RELATIONSHIPS**
**MEANINGFUL WORK**

I'm TORCHING…
**STUCKEDNESS**

I'm IGNITING…
**DREAMS**

I'm FUELING…
**ACTION**

I'm CRAVING…
**PURPOSE**

**NOTHING will extinguish my FIRE!**

Signed:_____  Date:_____

**Tribal Inventory**

Jim Rohn famously said, "You are the average of the 5 people you spend the most time with." If that is true, shouldn't we be actively aware of who is in our tribe? To do that, I've created something called a Tribal Inventory. A Tribal Inventory has 3 distinct stages and every tribe has 7 quintessential members. Take a look at the stages first to understand what happens in each step of the inventory. Then, read the tribe member descriptions below and decide who you currently have in your tribe that you could admire, who you are lacking and need to hire and who you need to put in a new role or remove from your tribe and fire.

**I. Admire**

There is a great Ted Talk called *Everyday Leadership* by Drew Dudley. Google his name or the title and it will be at the top. Well worth the 6-minute investment. In it, Drew talks about what he calls lollipop moments. Moments that other people have had with us or we have had with others that had a profound impact. He goes further to say that most of us have never shared with that person how impactful that lollipop moment was for us. We walk around with this memory of an experience of major significance, we may even tell the story to others, but we've never taken the time to tell the person who was the catalyst for that experience. I find the same is often true in our tribes. Those people you trust with your deepest secrets, with your kids, with your earthly possessions, with that phone call in the wee hours of the night—these are your tribe members. Some know it. Several don't. And why not? That is what Drew asks his viewers. Why don't we take the time to let these people know how much they mean to us? So now's the time. Send a text, write a letter, make a call. Be intentional about admiring those you can't imagine life without. Lollipop licked.

**II. Hire**

As you work through your tribal inventory, you may realize you are lacking some key members. How do you find these people if you don't have them? Look around. Neighborhood, work, church, LinkedIn, Facebook, parent group, gym. I have asked people that I meet, current friends and "suggested connections" on LinkedIn to be members of my tribe. I'm constantly looking to add to what I don't have. Sometimes it's as simple as a message via social media asking them to join and briefly describing why I need them in my tribe and what I'm hopeful they can help me with if they join. I connected with one tribe member on LinkedIn based on what his profile description was. I sent an invite to connect with a note about what I saw from his profile. I could see from his posts that he was both an Expert and Devil's Advocate. I invited him to coffee, confirmed my assumptions and asked him to be an Expert on a certain area in my tribe and he agreed. I see him about once a quarter and our conversations always leave me pondering on things I hadn't considered. The right ones will say yes. Most are flattered you considered them in the first place. It's amazing what happens when you ask.

### III. Fire

You may have people in your tribe that hold you back because of their own jealousy, pride, arrogance, hurt feelings, selfishness or whatever. You may have people that you have continually gone to for support only to be bludgeoned by questions and criticism. These people could be your parents, friends, co-workers, or maybe even your spouse. As you think about your interactions with these tribe members and the descriptions from earlier, ask yourself if they are in the right role in your tribe. More often than not, you will find your "firing" of a tribe member is not a removal from your tribe altogether, but more of a shift in roles. You may discover that your Dreamer is really a Devil's advocate. Going to them when you are dreaming big dreams is disastrous because they poke holes in everything. Move them to the role of Devil's Advocate and bring them options. Lay those options before them and allow them to do what they do best—find all the reasons it won't work. The best part about this is your firing them from one role and hiring them in another doesn't have to be a formal exchange. You simply make the switch in the future and use them when their role and gifts will be most effective.

There may, however, be some circumstances where people need to be fired from your tribe altogether. I'm not saying you cut these people out of your life completely, but rather look at how they love and support you. Or don't. If it's not what you need, then you have a difficult decision to make. Sometimes this will require a tough conversation to let this person know you can't be around them any longer. Other times this may simply be a choice not to call or otherwise engage someone who has historically been critical and unsupportive of you.

All seven roles are essential in your tribe. They all have a part and you need ALL of them. Yes, some of these can be filled by the same people. You may also have several people filling one role, but I find it best to have separate individuals for each. You could also have several under one category. You might have one or two listeners compared to five connectors. The combinations are endless. You may also have other roles according to your own purpose, but I find that these roles are must-haves.

One other potential outcome of this exercise could be what one of my clients experienced that I never expected. She told me in going through the Tribal Inventory she realized that she didn't have a tribe—at all! Instead, she was fulfilling several of these roles for several different people based on their needs. Suddenly it made sense why she was exhausted all the time and felt like she had no support. She quickly put this exercise to work for her and fired a number of people that were draining her and started hiring a supportive and affirming tribe!

**Listener**—This is the person that you spill your ideas to in a spastic and chaotic stream of consciousness. They follow you down every rabbit hole and take all the detours along the way. They may ask clarifying questions along the way to understand you better and to help you build clarity as you think out loud. But mostly, they are quiet. This tribe member doesn't offer advice or try to solve for Y. When you are out of breath at the end and ask, "Ya know what I mean?" They shake their head yes with knowing certainty. Mostly though, They. Just. Listen.

| Current Tribe Member(s) | Potential Hire | Potential Fire |
|---|---|---|
| _____ | _____ | _____ |
| _____ | _____ | _____ |
| _____ | _____ | _____ |

**Dreamer**—This tribe member loves to start their sentences with, "What if…" They take your idea and push it to the edge of possibility. Their ideas are larger than life and often fuel your own ideas to grow into spaces you wouldn't dare go on your own. We walk away from our time with them on an adrenaline rush and mind full of new and exciting ideas. Typically, they don't have any ideas on the practical end and that's ok because their job is to DREAM. BIG!

| Current Tribe Member(s) | Potential Hire | Potential Fire |
|---|---|---|
| _____ | _____ | _____ |
| _____ | _____ | _____ |
| _____ | _____ | _____ |

**Devil's Advocate**—A quintessential member of the tribe that is often avoided—on purpose. They are also the most misunderstood. They poke holes in plans and dreams because they can't help it. Their mind is just wired that way. They are drawn to all the scenarios that will never happen and all the reasons your dream is going to go up in a cloud of smoke. They are basically your WhatIfAbouts with skin on… "Have you thought doing that another way?" "I'm not sure that will work." "Try looking at it like this." "What about X? And if X happens what will you do with Y?" They aren't trying to rain on your parade, they simply want the best for you and this is their way of showing it. Timing for engagement of the Devil's Advocate is key. Bringing them in at the beginning can be a dream killer, but bringing them in once the plans are drawn out can be a solid dose of necessary reality.

| Current Tribe Member(s) | Potential Hire | Potential Fire |
|---|---|---|
| _____ | _____ | _____ |
| _____ | _____ | _____ |
| _____ | _____ | _____ |

**Organizer**—What comes first, second and third is this tribe member's specialty. They thrive on details and "the little stuff" that are necessary to make reality, well, reality. They take the chaos of the swarm of ideas and deliver it in a well-organized step-by-step package. They think about the sequence as well as the resources needed of both people and time. They have their planners out, their post-it notes and a multiplicity of pens and markers. "So here's how we should start and then after that, we'll do this and that will get us ready for the next step…" When meeting with them we can put, "Oh yeah, I didn't think about that" on repeat.

| Current Tribe Member(s) | Potential Hire | Potential Fire |
|---|---|---|
| _____ | _____ | _____ |
| _____ | _____ | _____ |
| _____ | _____ | _____ |

**Catalyst**—They throw down the gauntlet or give you that extra push over the hill. However you describe the catalyst, they are the ones that give legs to that "next step". They give you an assignment and a deadline and assure you they will be there to check on your progress, and then they show up and check on your progress! In fact, they're a little obsessive about it/borderline annoying, but we love them for it! While discussing the idea of writing *Fire Starters*, my catalyst said, "OK, let's set a meeting in 4 weeks and you will come prepared with the intro to your book written and an outline for all of your chapters." This was all I needed. I had all of that done in 2 days! Turns out I just needed a challenge from my catalyst.

| Current Tribe Member(s) | Potential Hire | Potential Fire |
|---|---|---|
| _____ | _____ | _____ |
| _____ | _____ | _____ |
| _____ | _____ | _____ |

**Connector**—This tribe member can be inserted multiple times throughout the process. They have a network and aren't afraid to use it. Their comments after listening to you might include, "You know, you need to talk to. . .this person" or "You should meet with my friend . . . who does. . . " They get excited when their tribe gets connected b/c it grows their tribe and connections, and that's what connectors are all about. Connectors also love to share resources. "Have you read this book?" "Do you know about this podcast?" "Have you ever been to this event?" These are common questions connectors will ask you between the flurry of introductions they are making and scheduling on your behalf.

**Current Tribe Member(s)**　　**Potential Hire**　　**Potential Fire**

_____　　_____　　_____

_____　　_____　　_____

_____　　_____　　_____

---

**Expert**--the expert is the one who has already arrived at the place you are trying to go. They are a mentor. They have the inside track on where you are going. They know the life hacks to accelerate your growth and success, and strategically hold back certain pieces until you are ready, thus enabling you to learn from the experience yourself. They are simultaneously your biggest fans and your biggest challengers. "What do you think might happen if you tweaked X?" "Have you ever thought about Z and how that might change things if you did?" They know the answers, but they are leading you to discover on your own. They're guiding without telling or pushing their own agenda because they want to see YOU succeed. You leave every conversation with the expert feeling confident and energized to take your project to the next level.

**Current Tribe Member(s)**　　**Potential Hire**　　**Potential Fire**

_____　　_____　　_____

_____　　_____　　_____

_____　　_____　　_____

Made in the USA
Columbia, SC
12 August 2024